This Coloring Book Belongs To:

....

GRAFFITI

COLORING BOOK

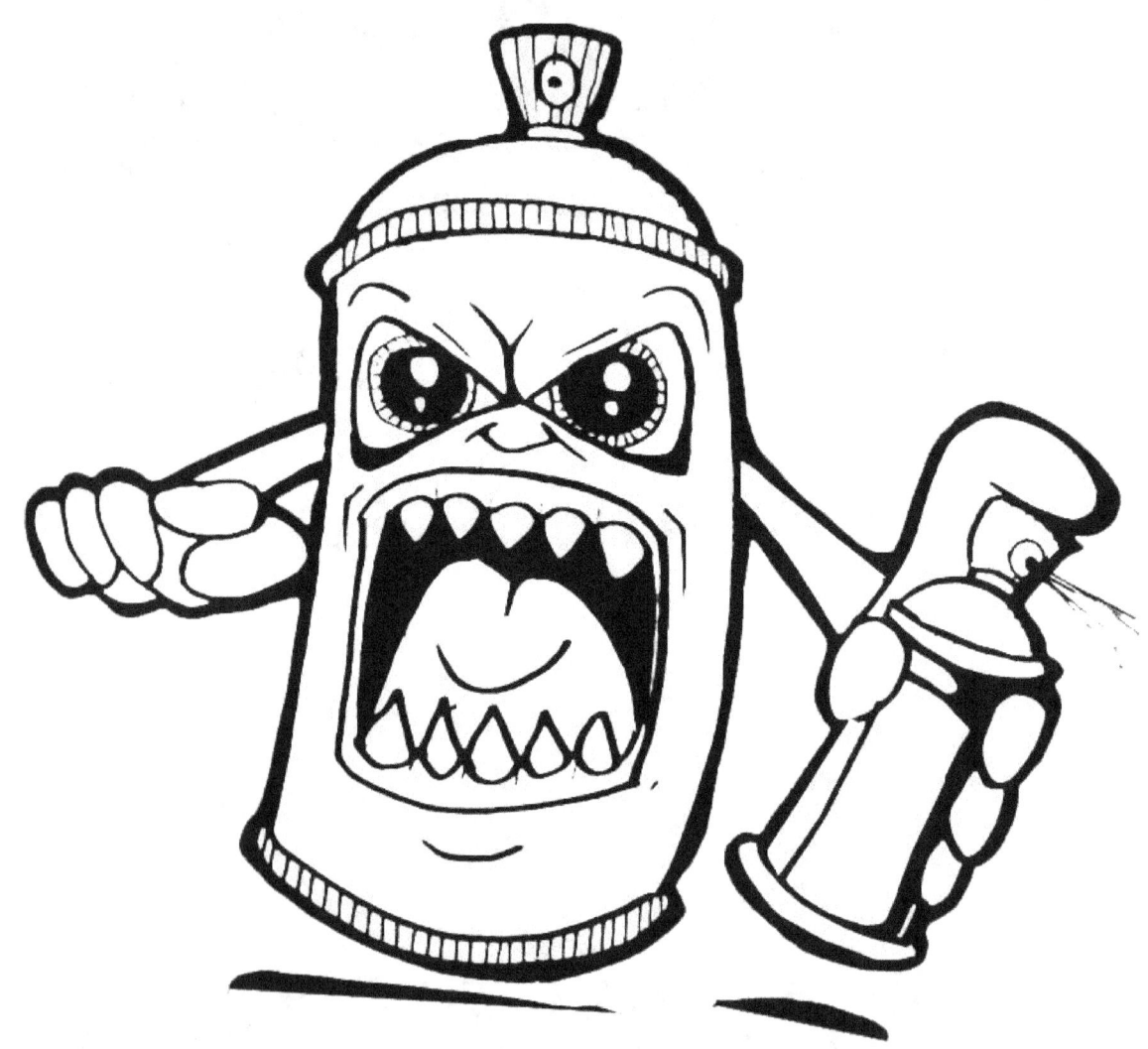

Copyright © Funny Art Press
All rights reserved. No part of this publication may be copied,
Reproduced in any format, by any means, electronic or otherwise,
Without prior consent from the copyright owner and publisher of this book

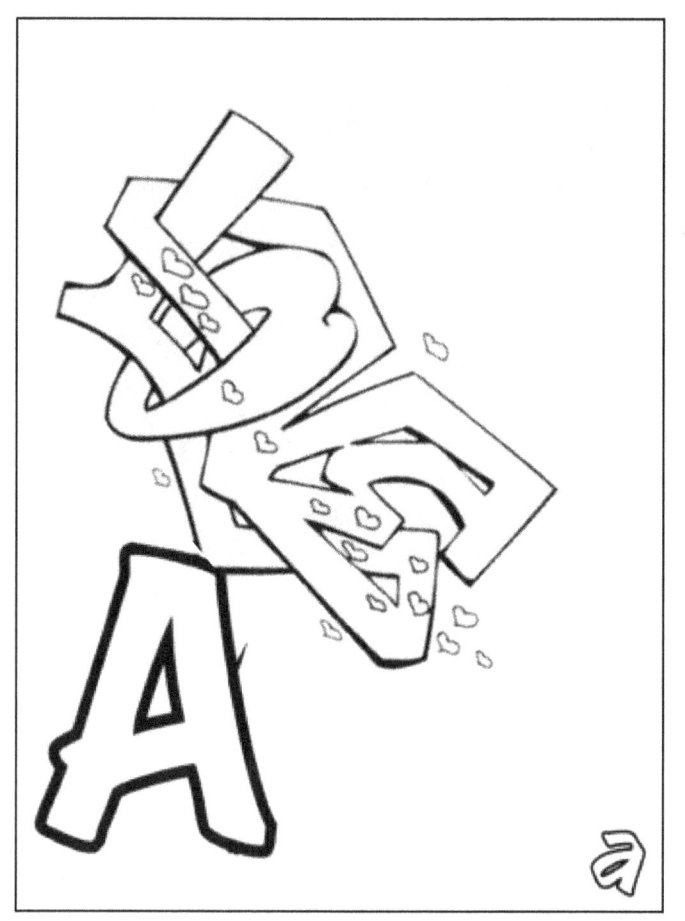
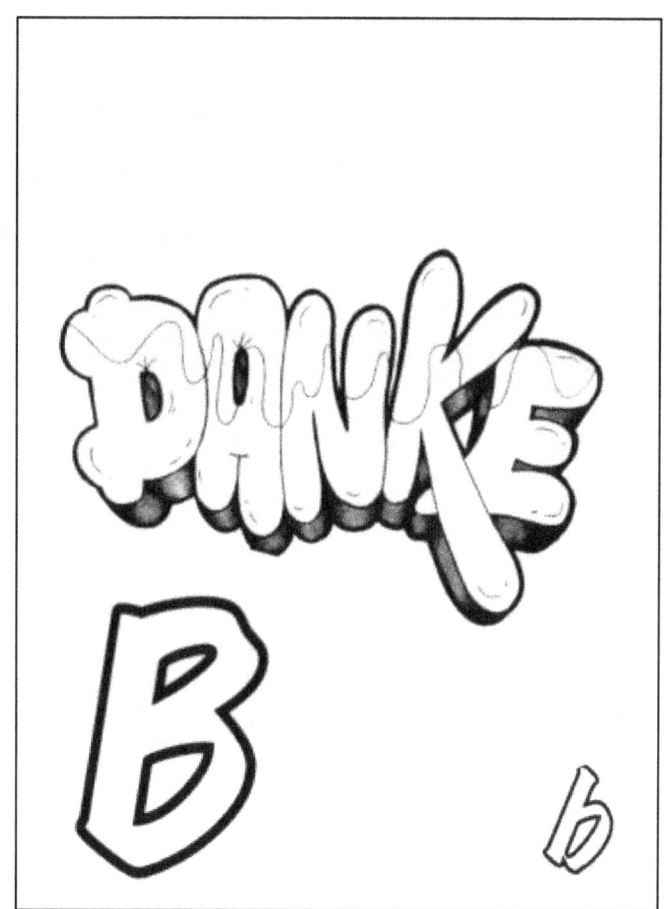
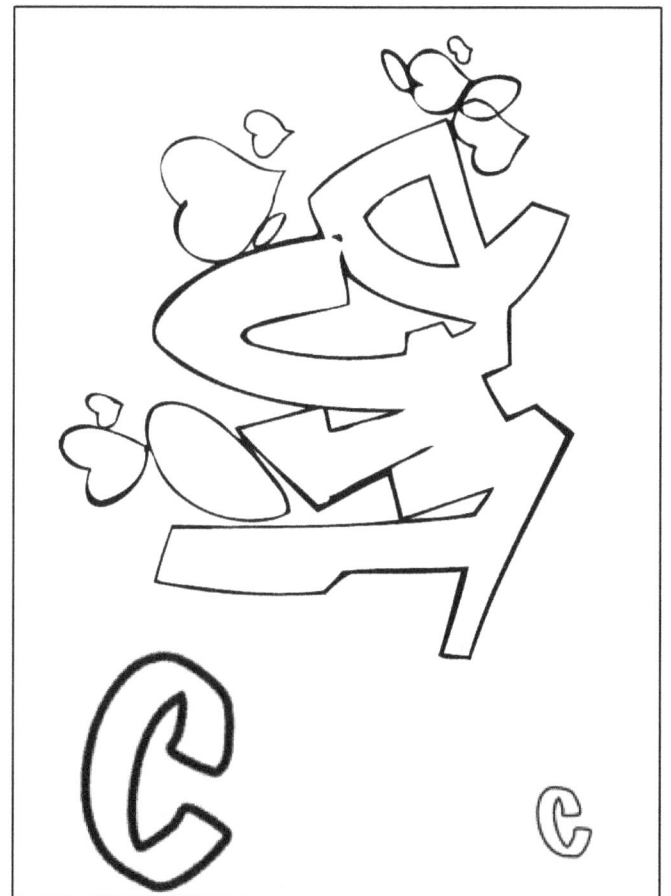
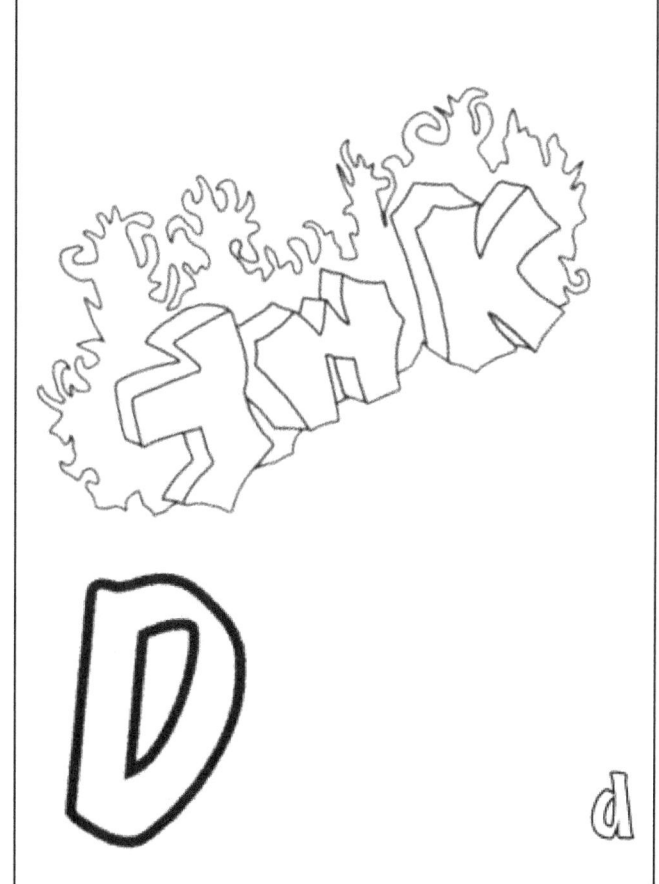

TEST COLOR PAGE
CHECK HOW YOUR COLORS SHOW OUR PAPER HERE

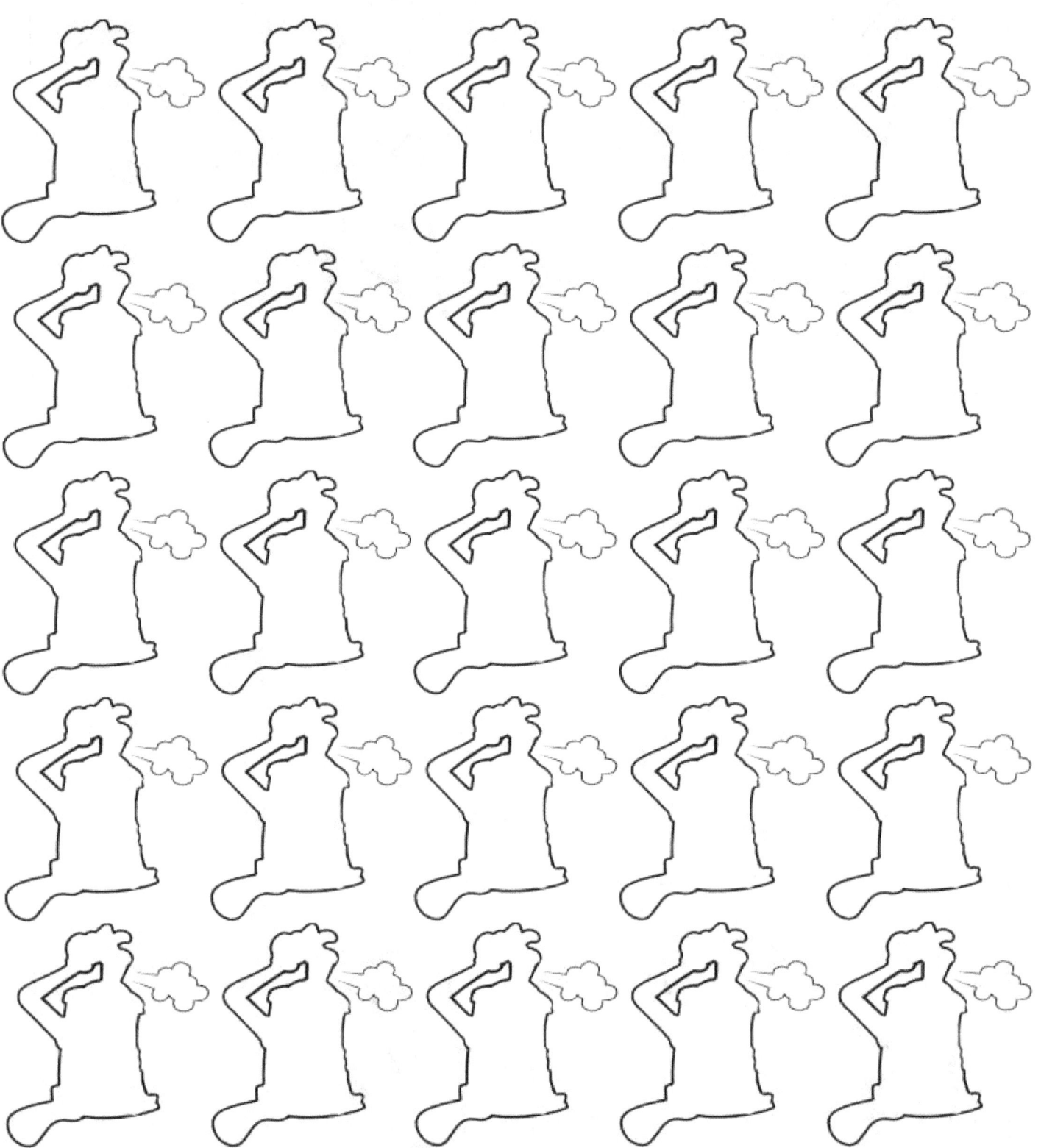

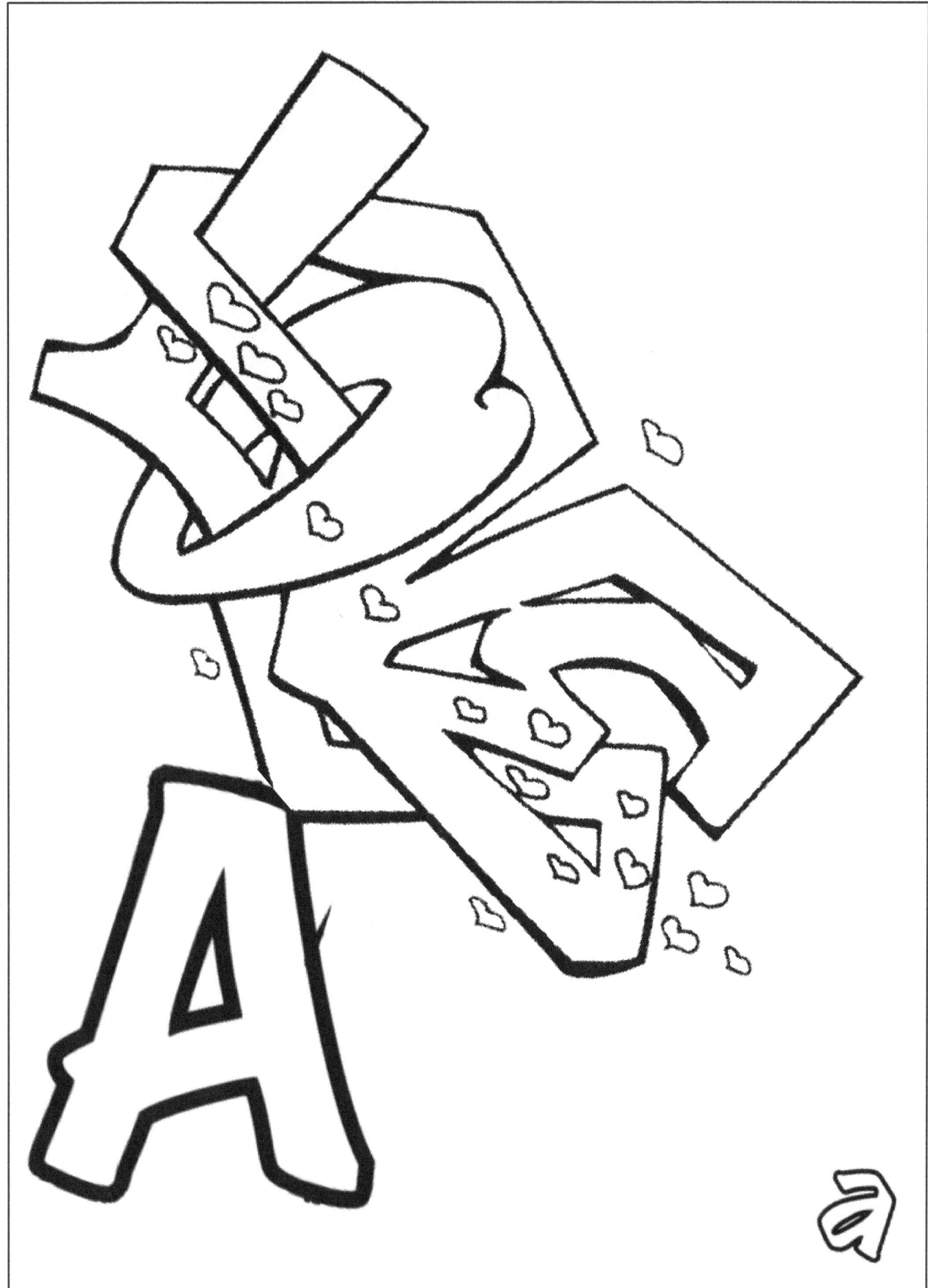

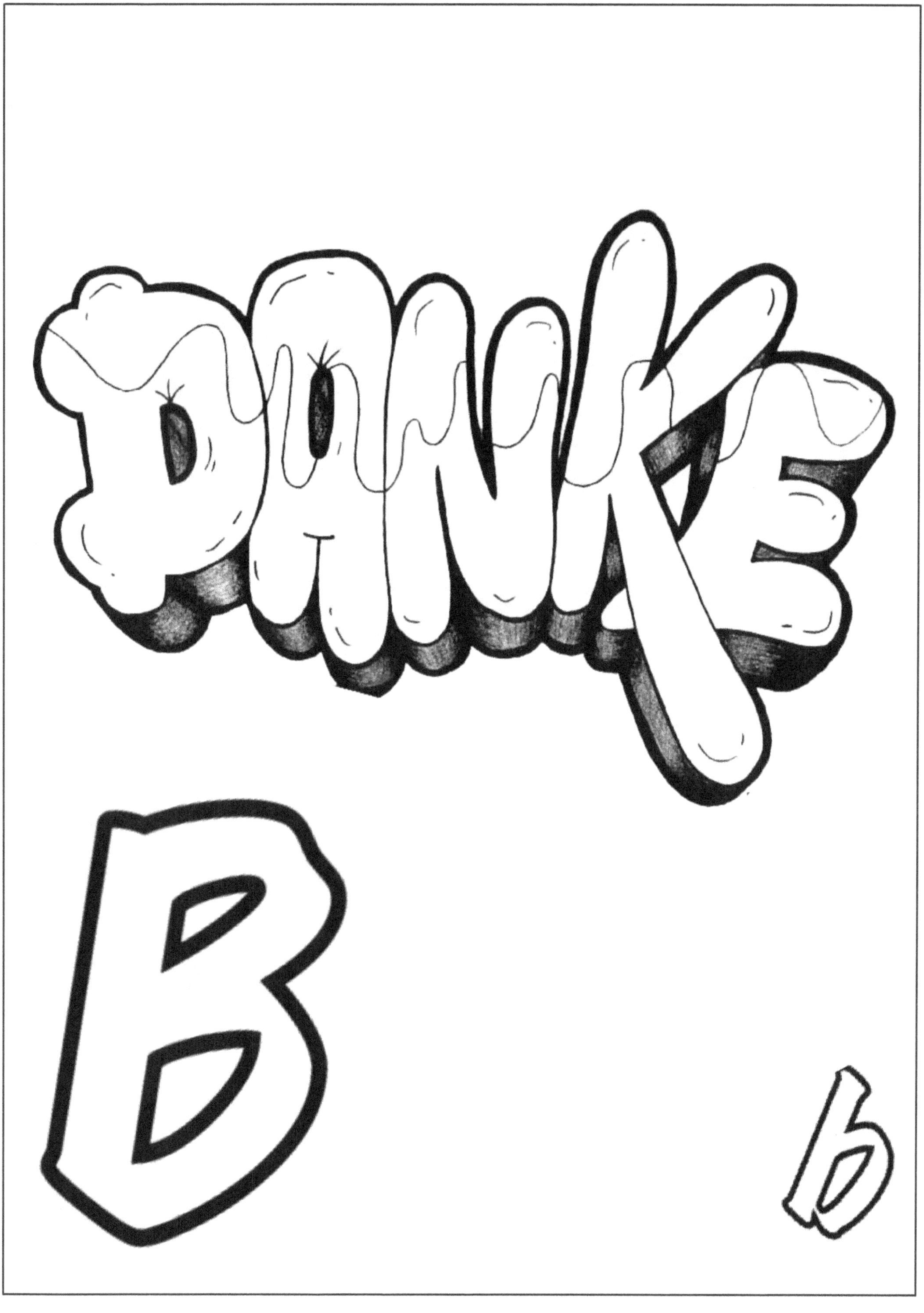

DANKE

B

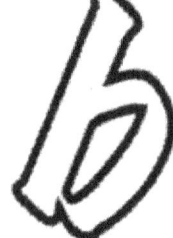

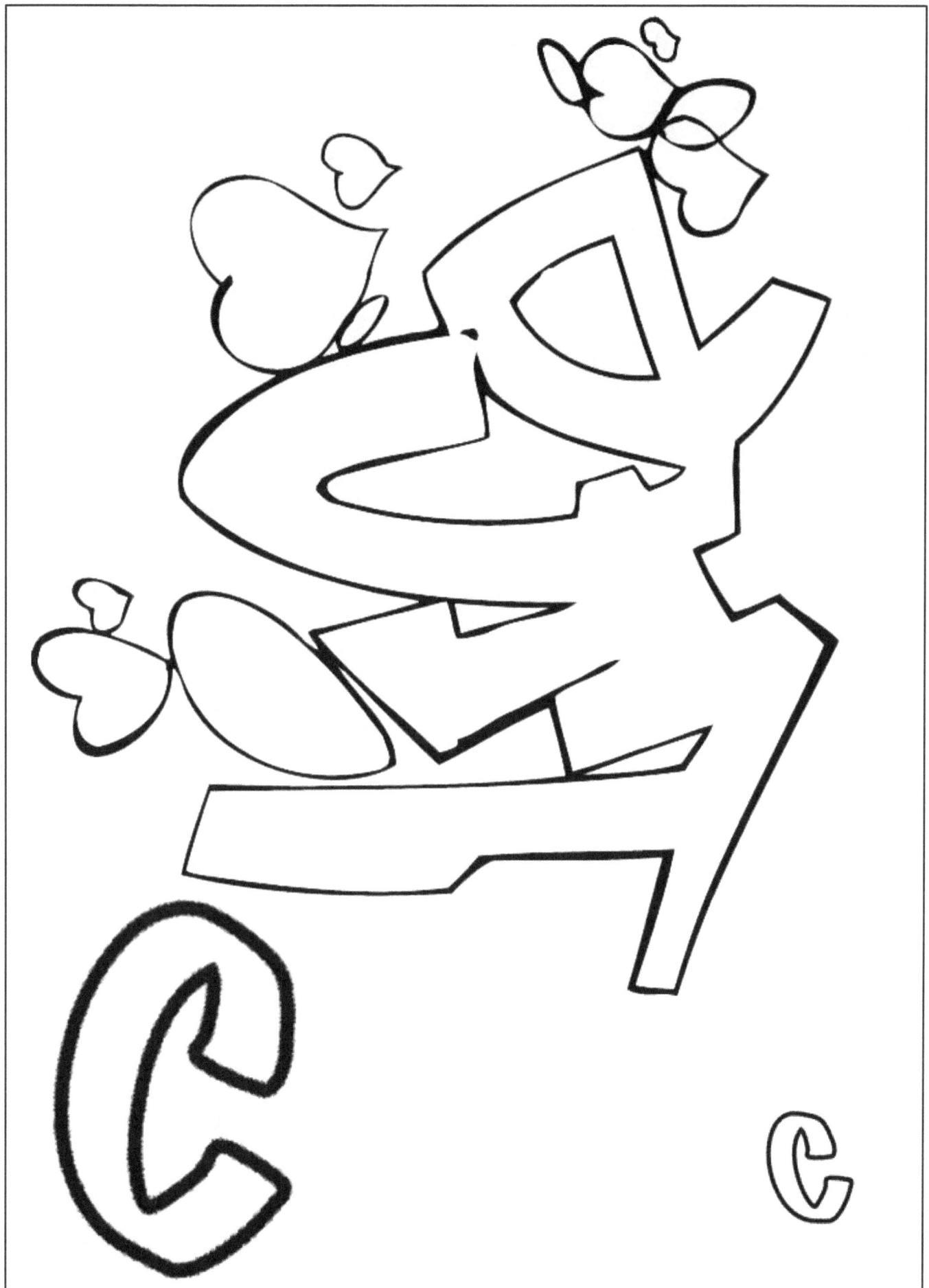

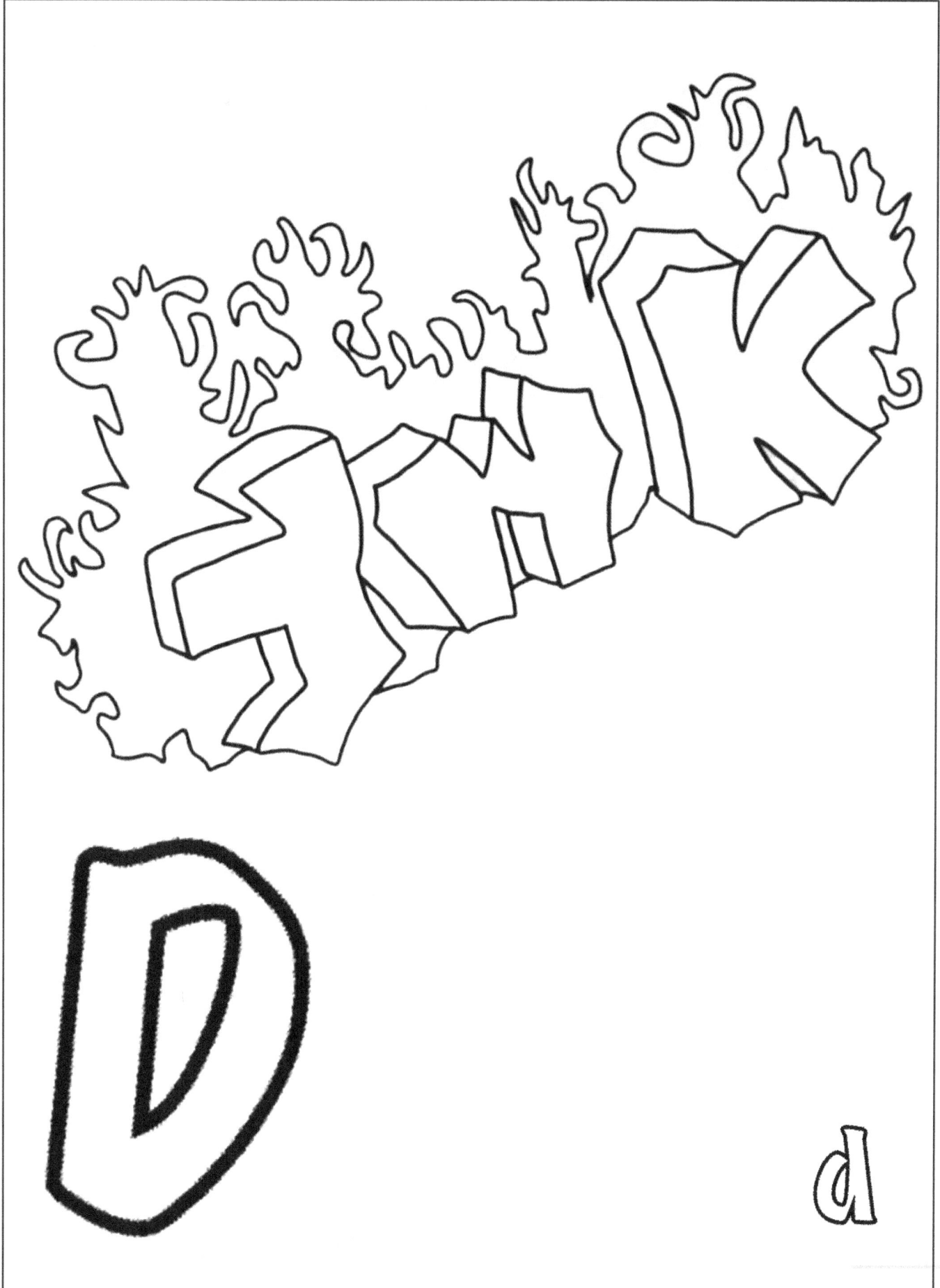

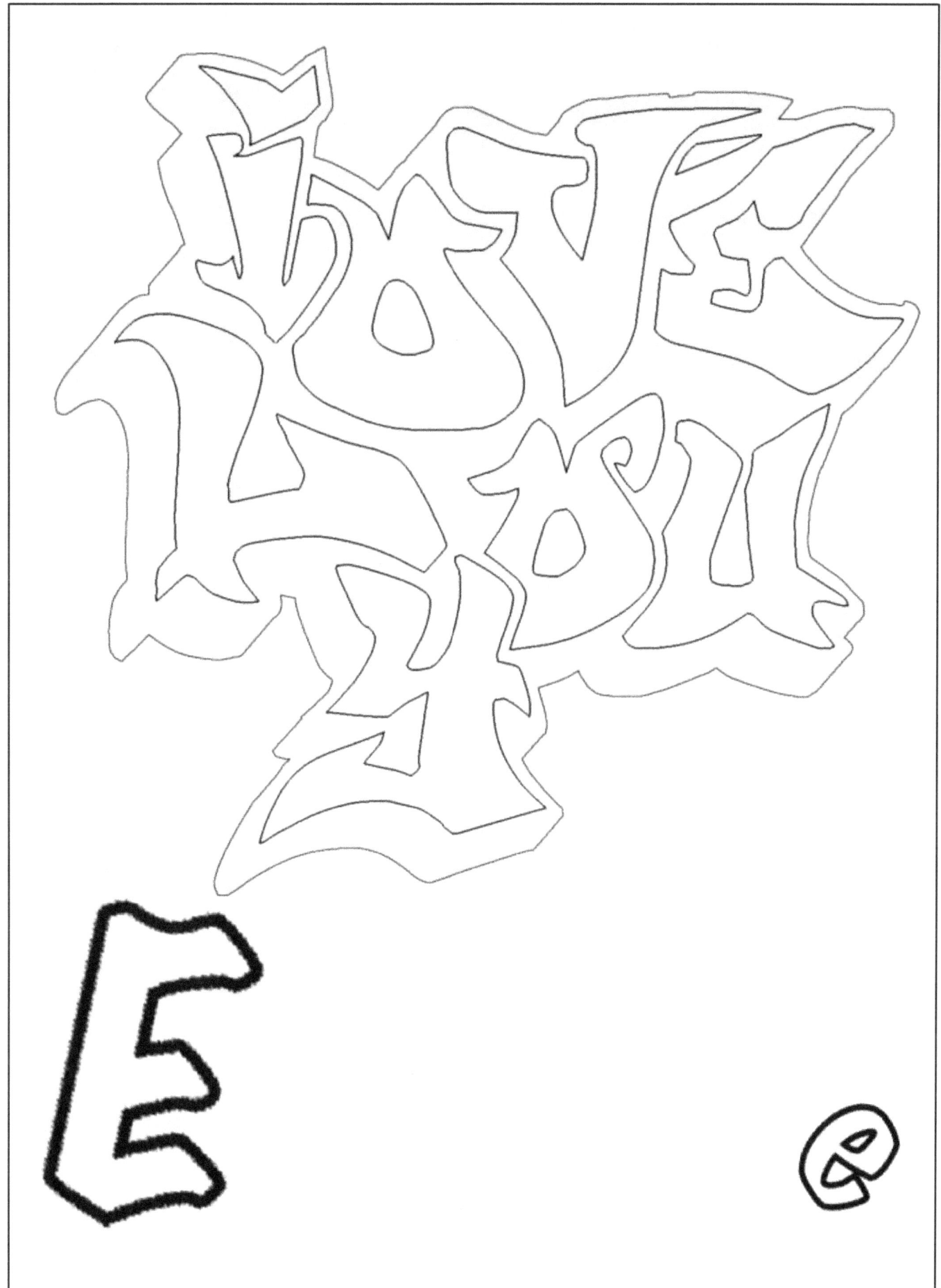

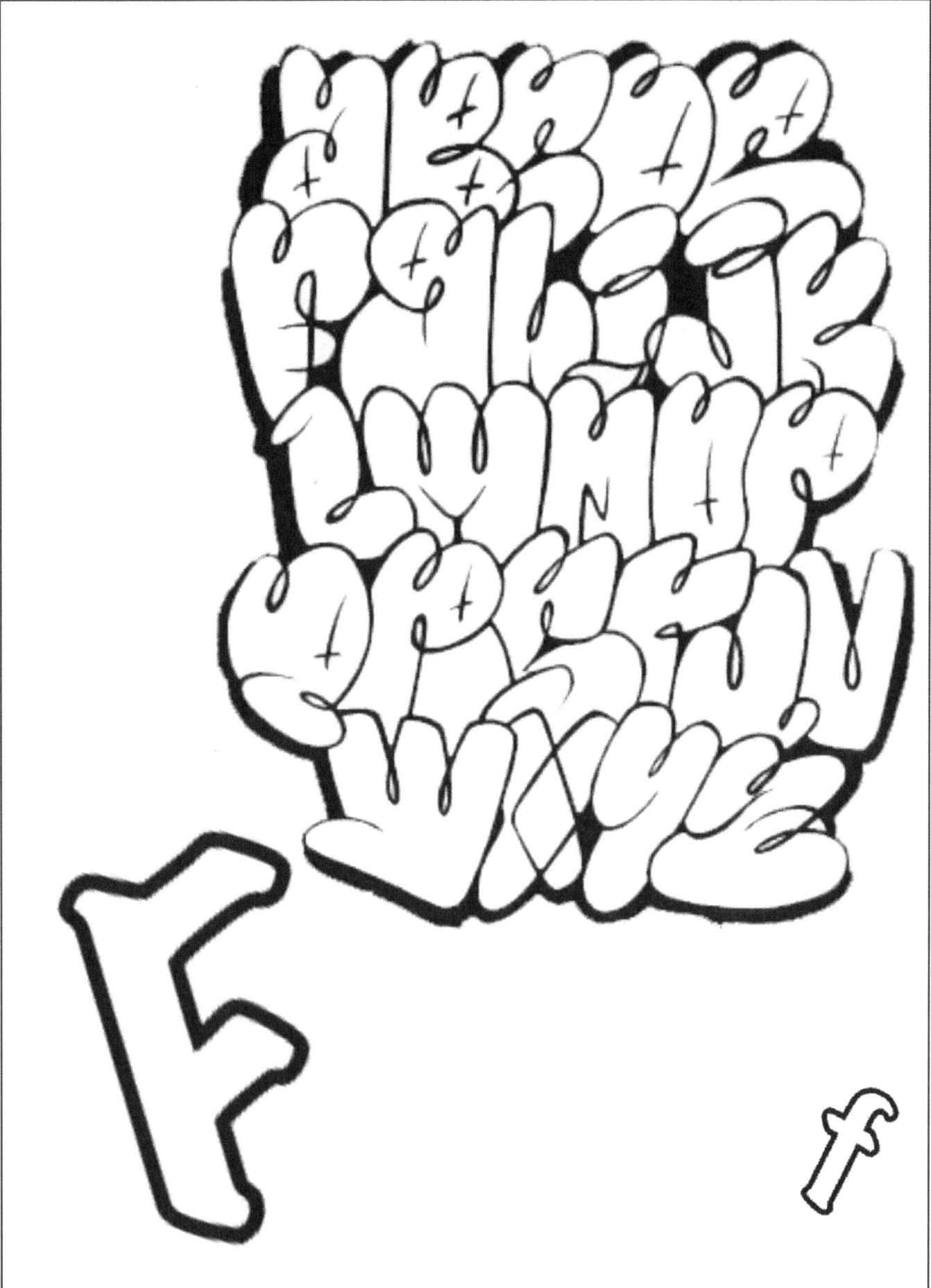

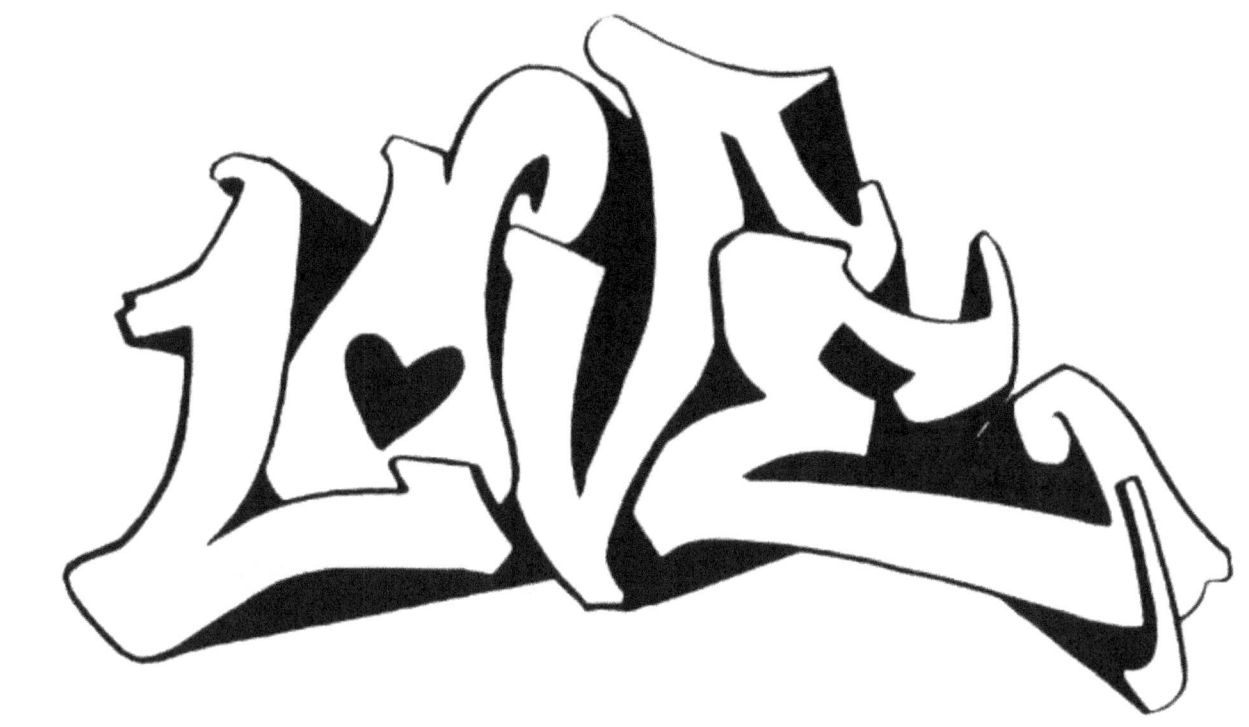

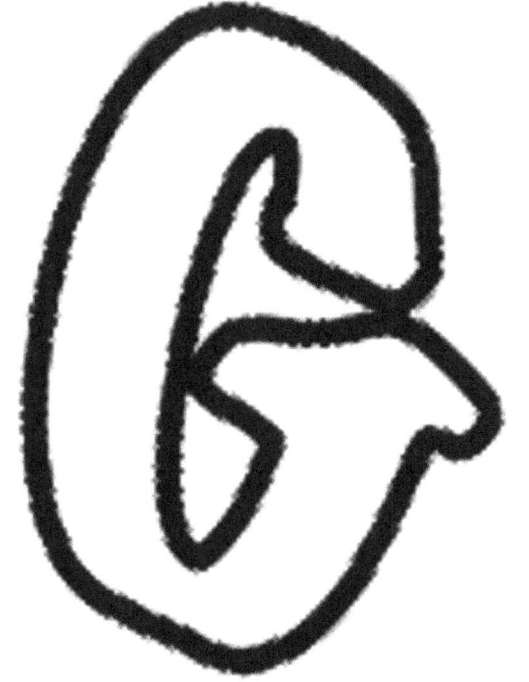

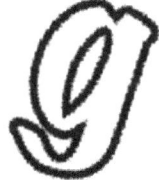

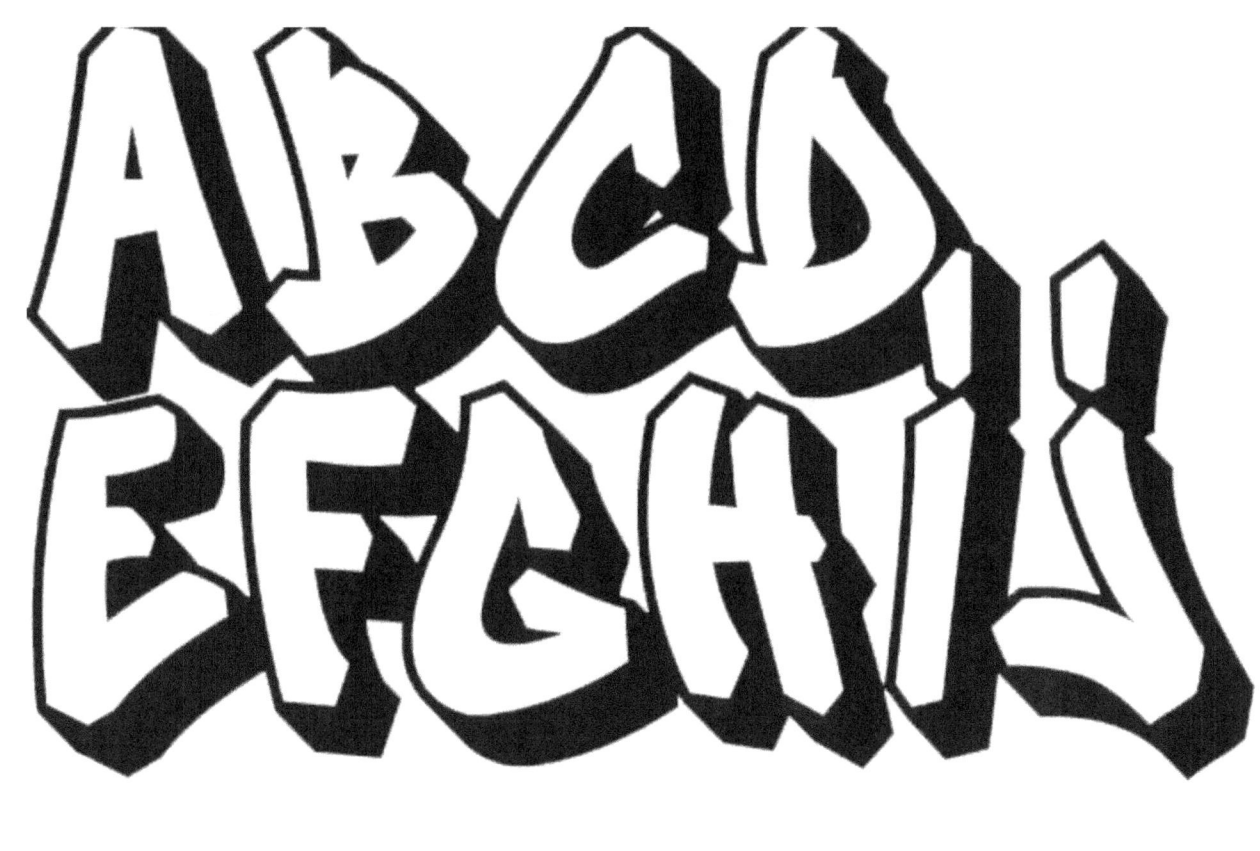

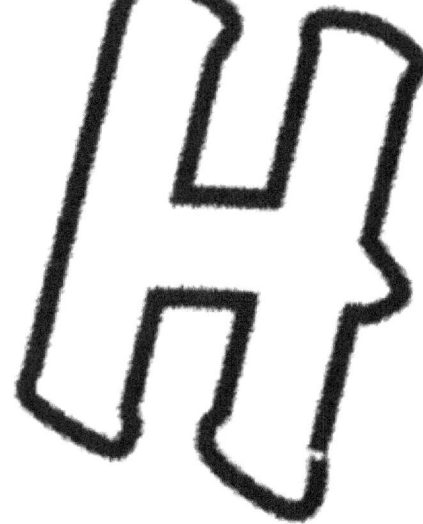

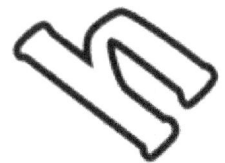

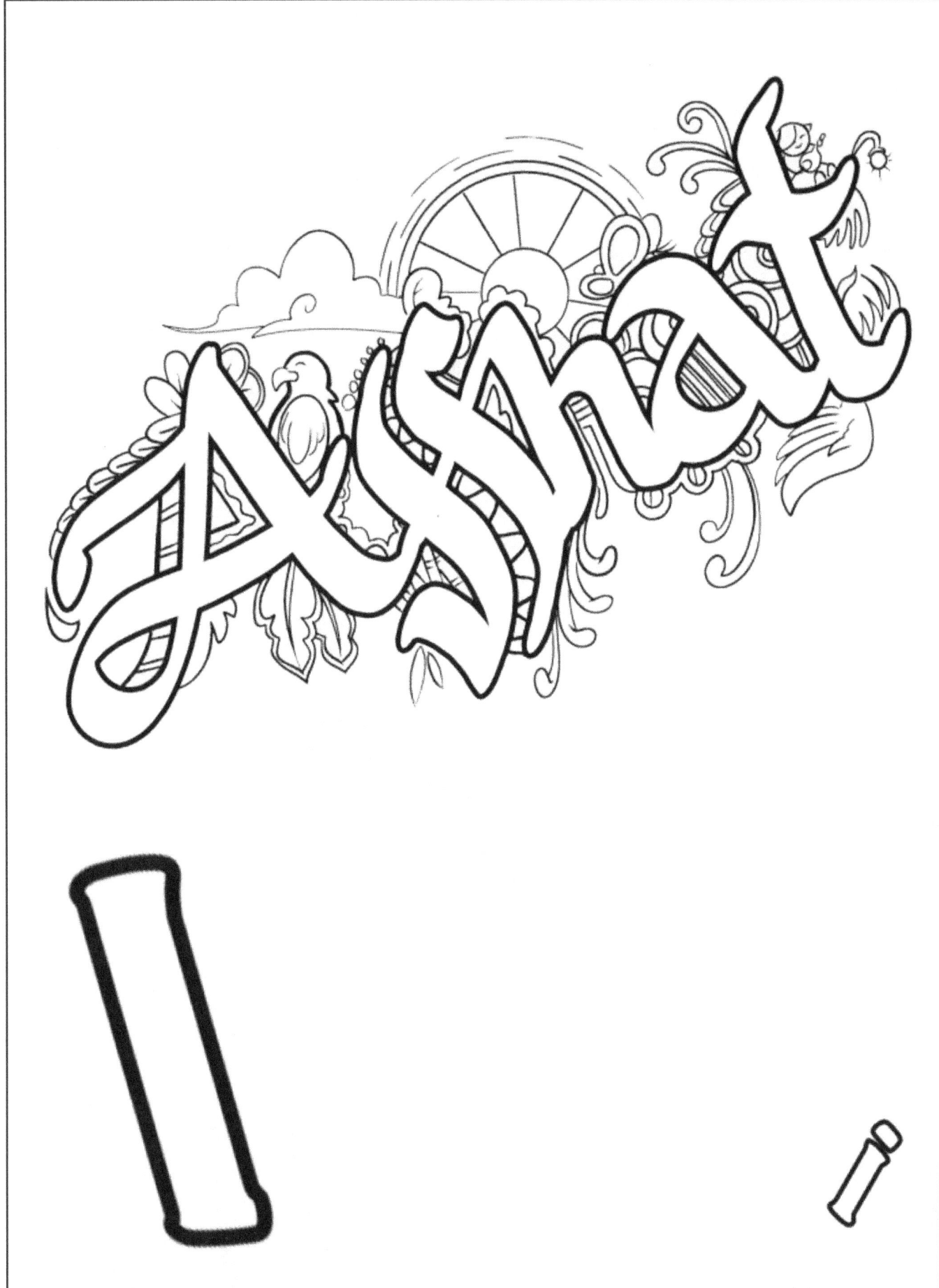

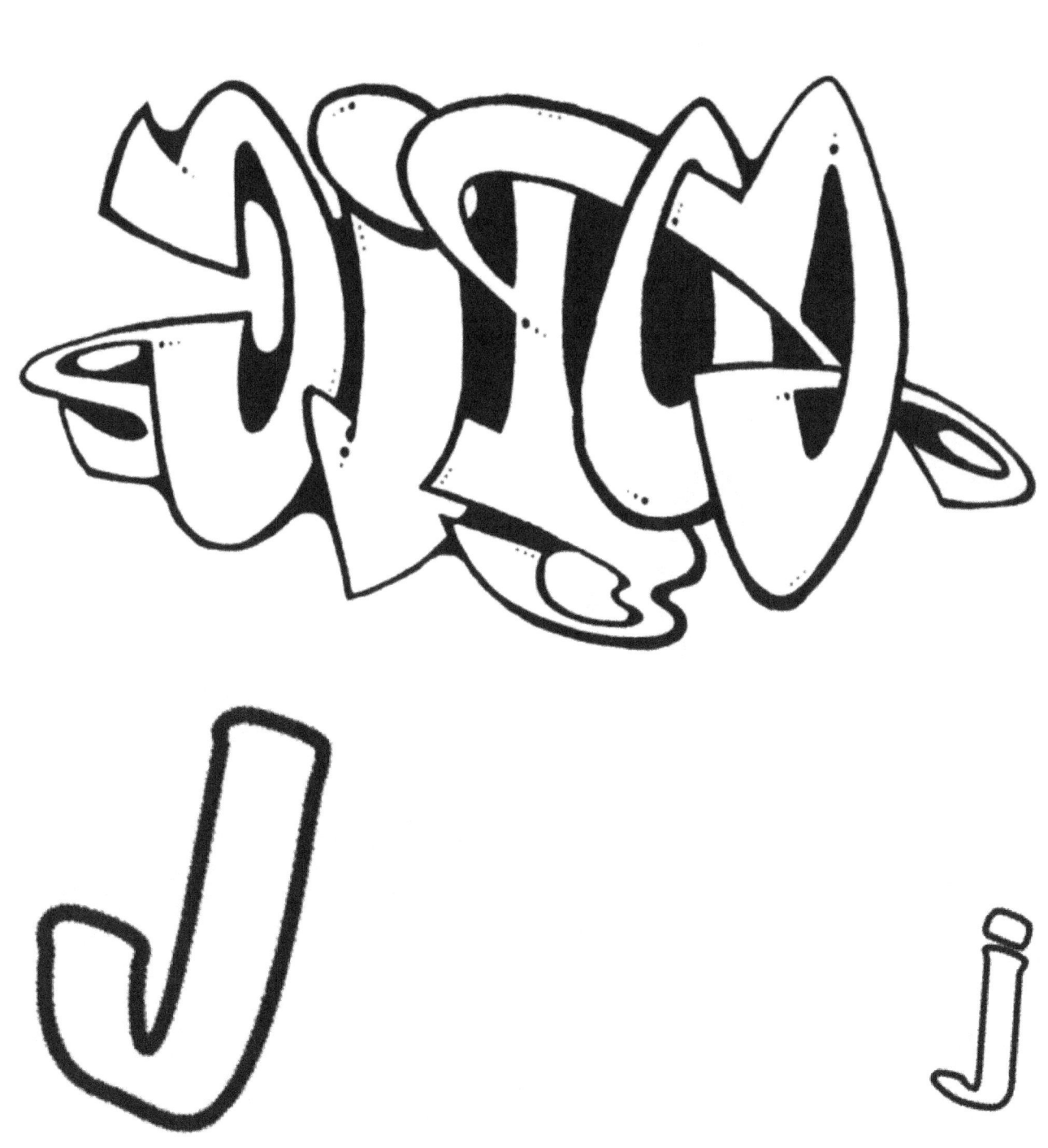

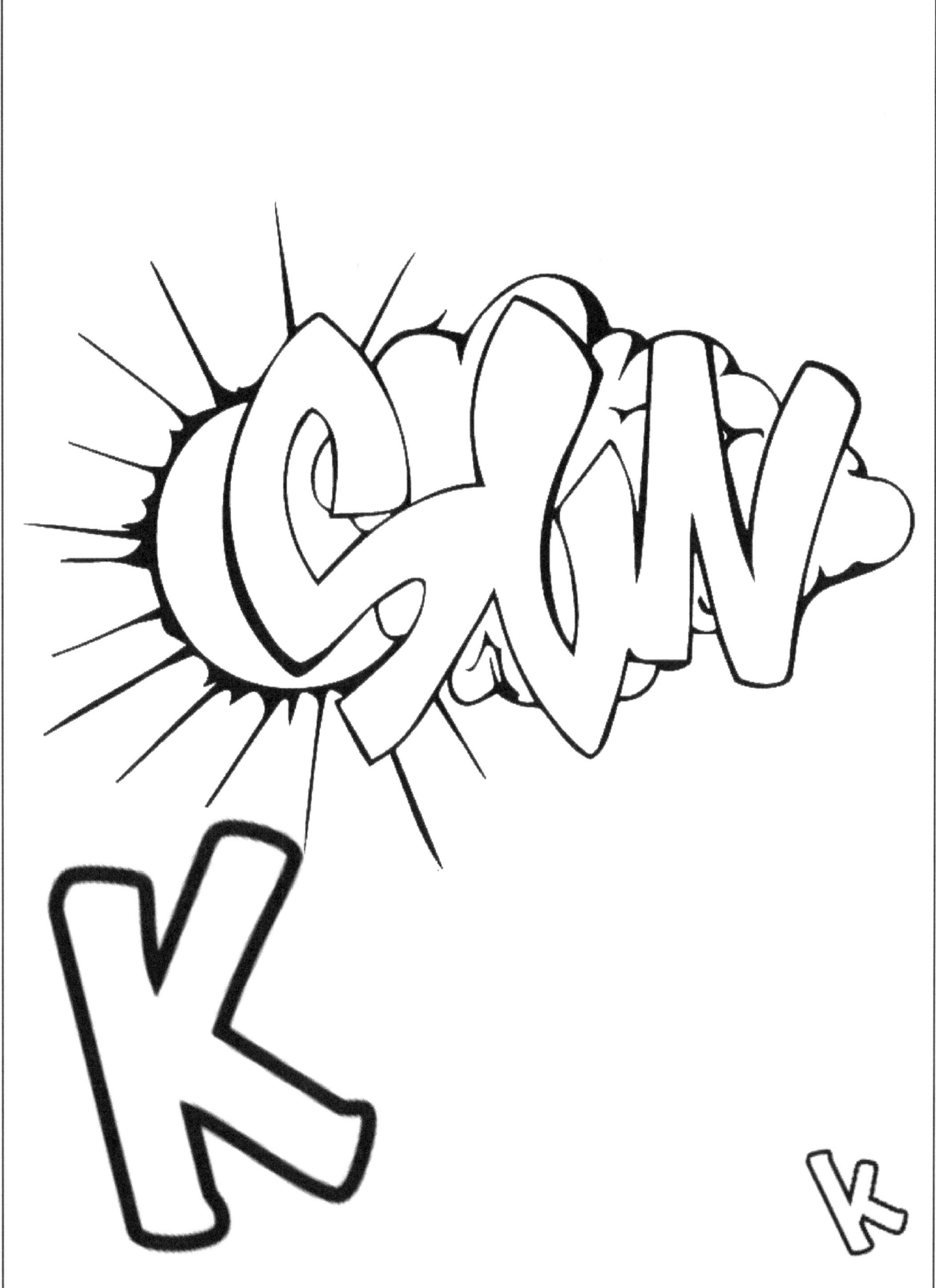

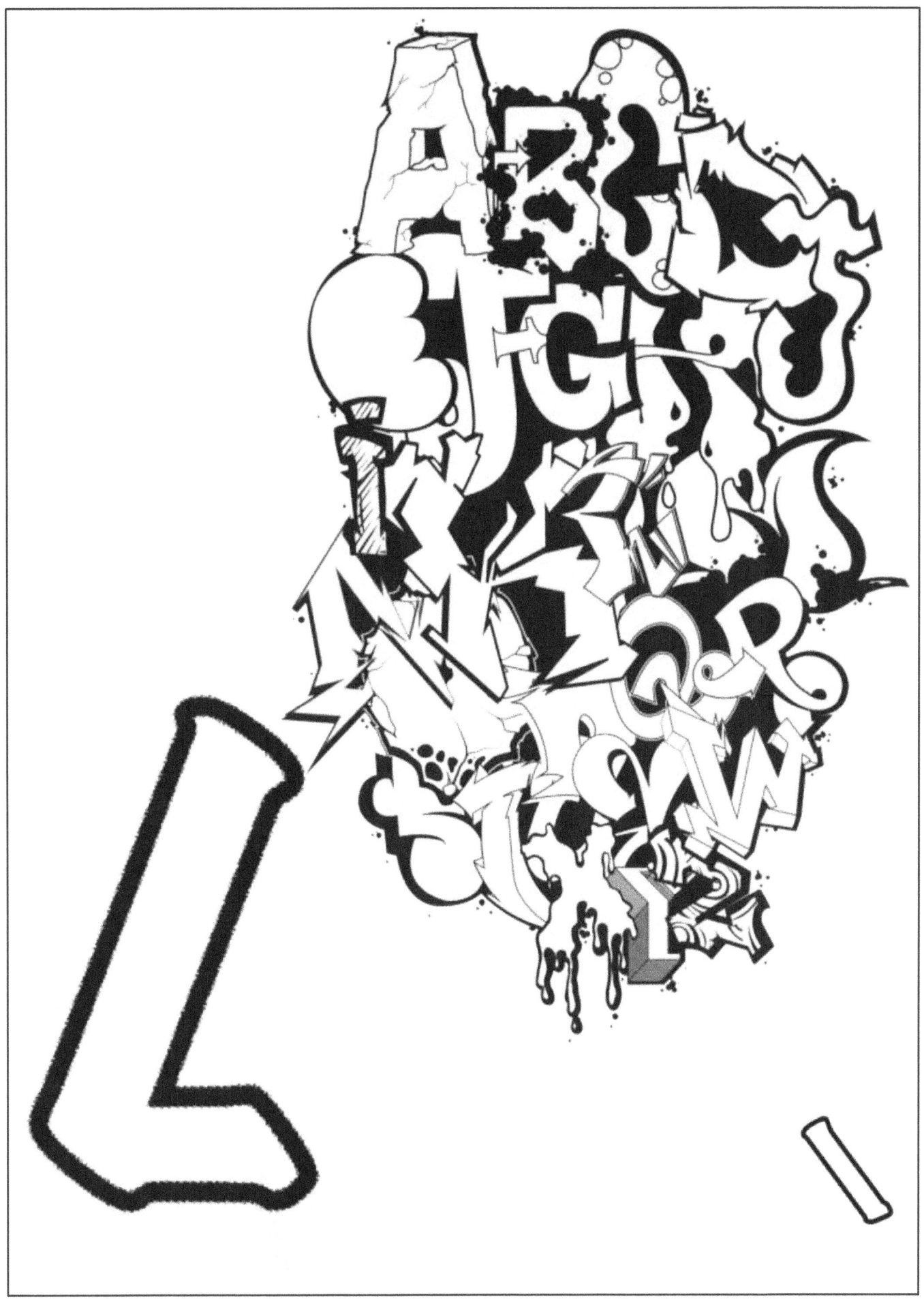

MNFST.

M

m

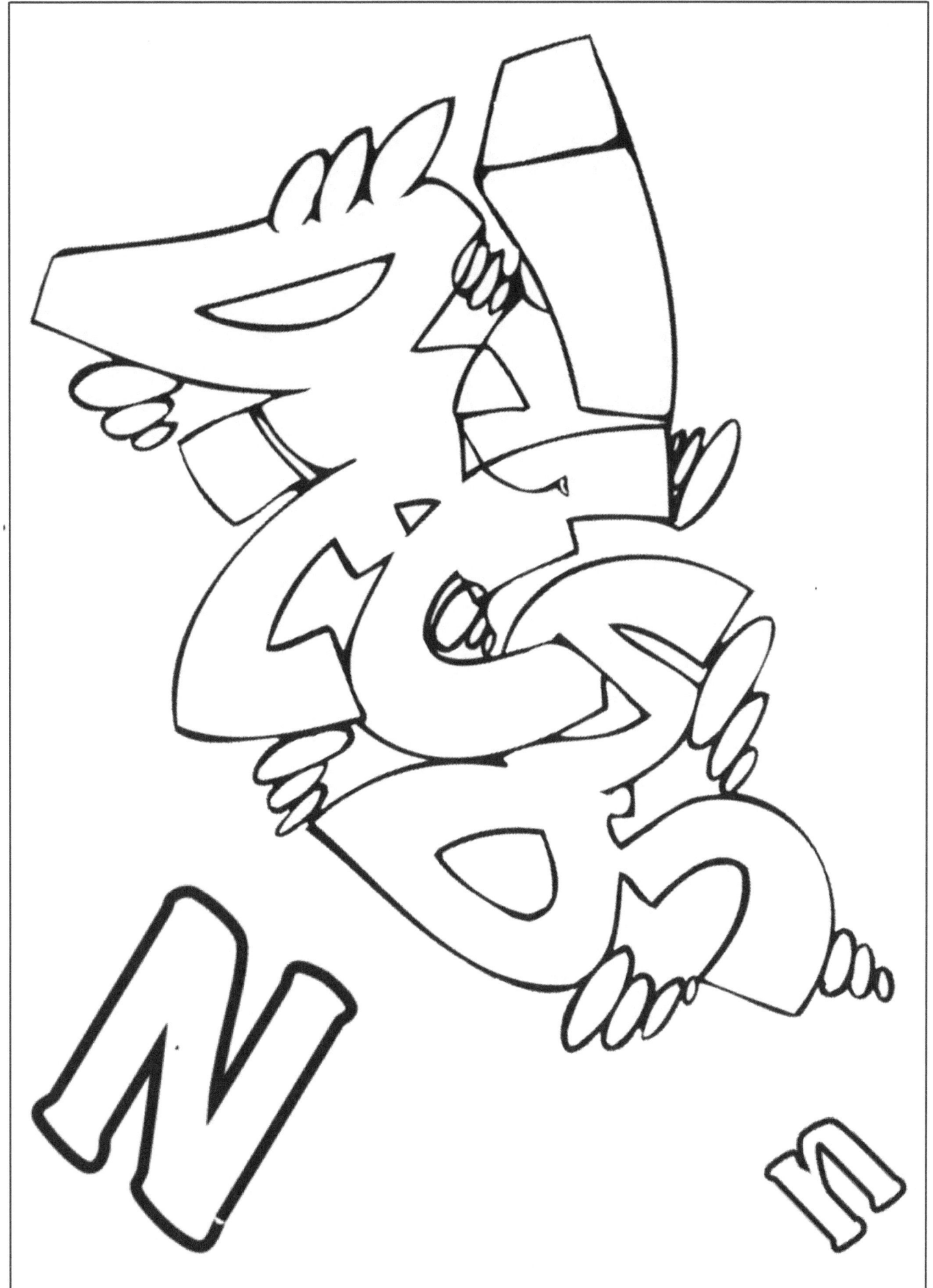

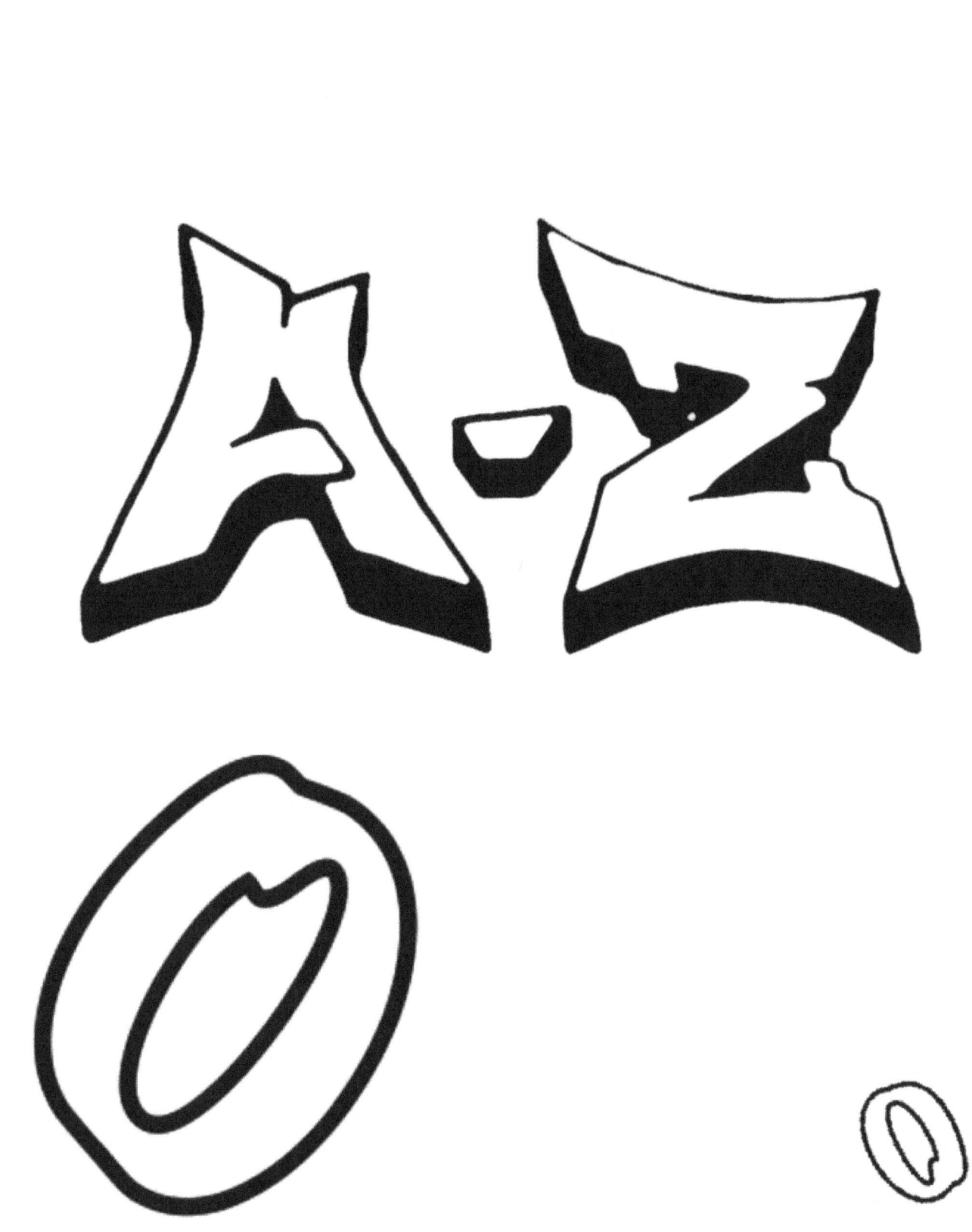

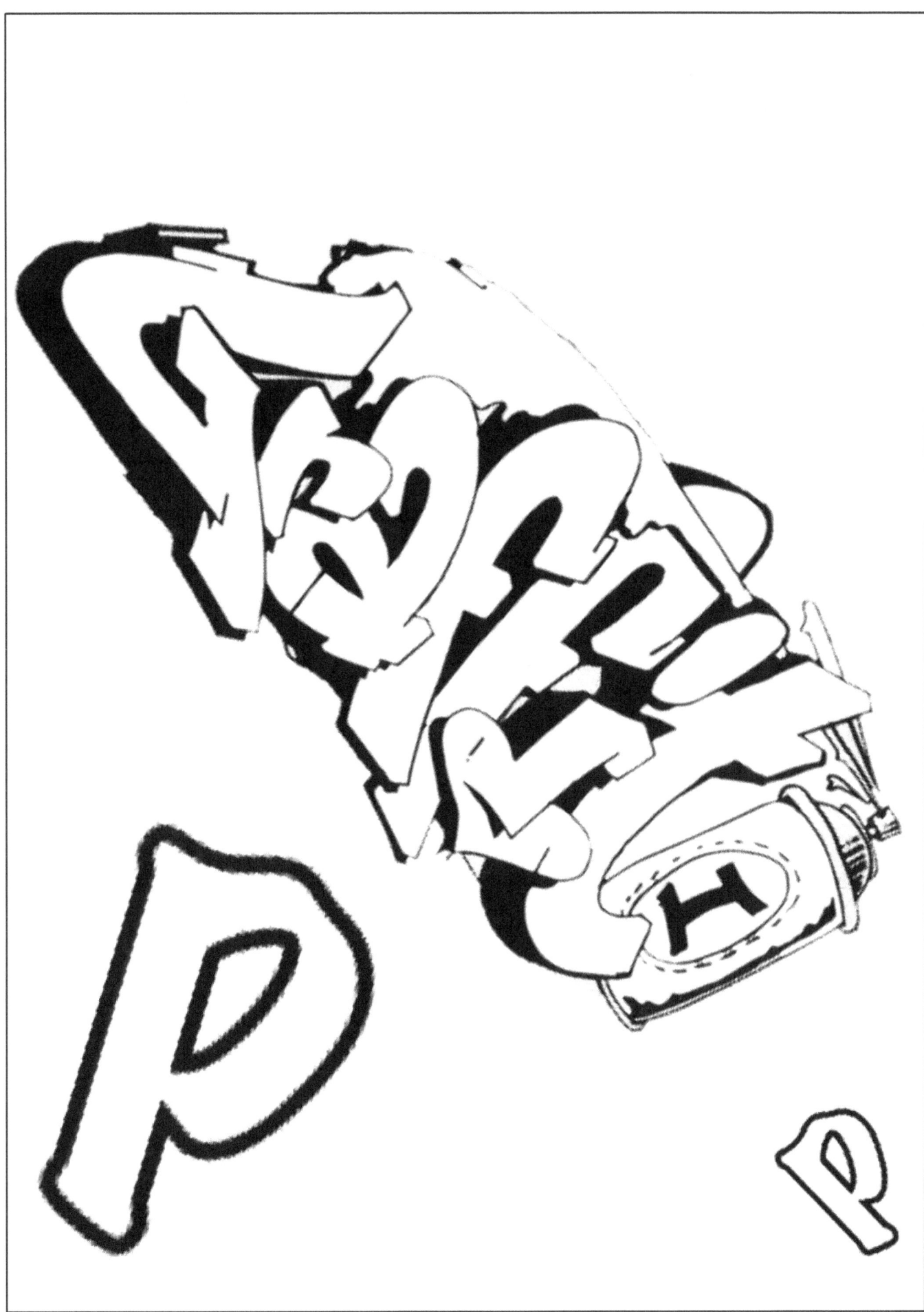

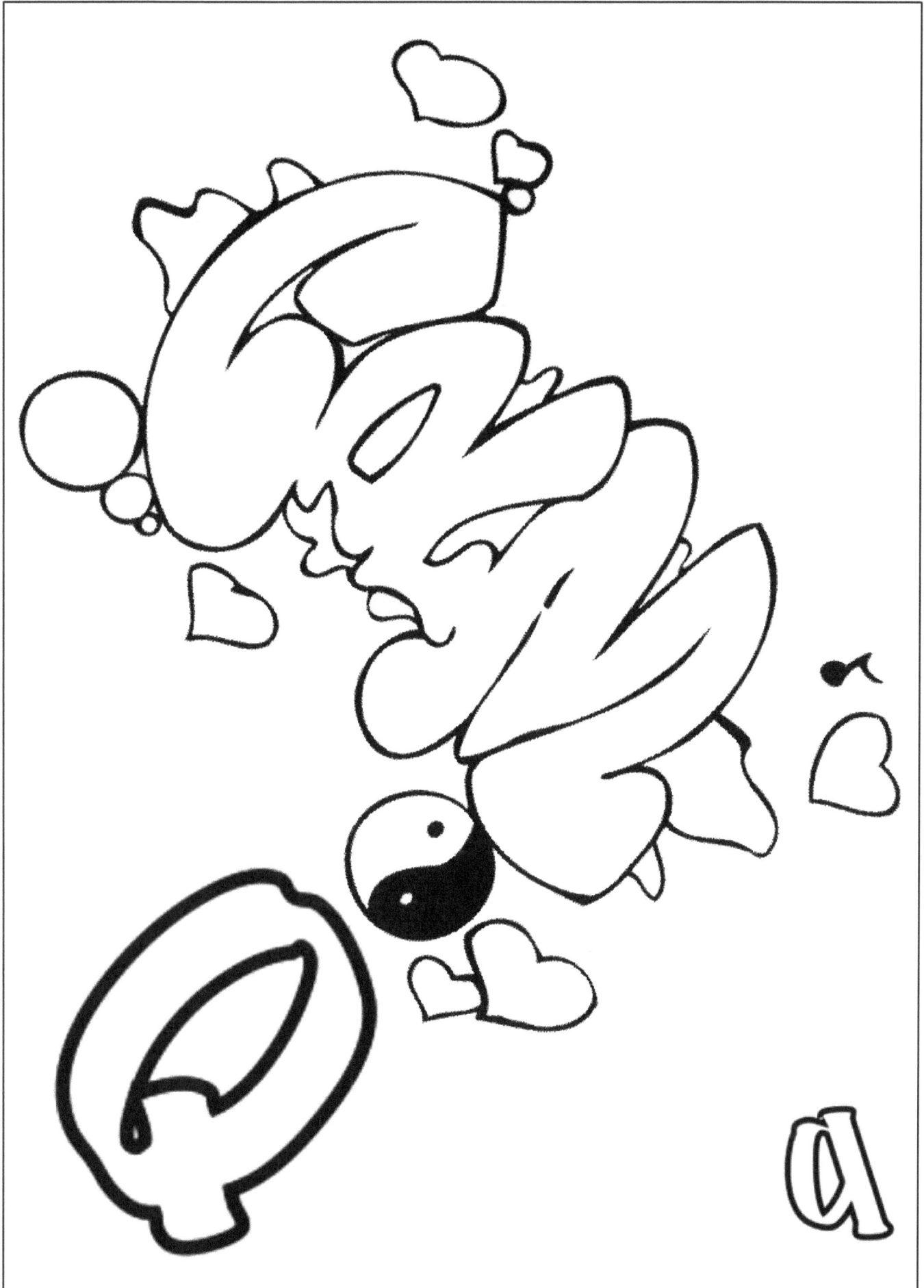

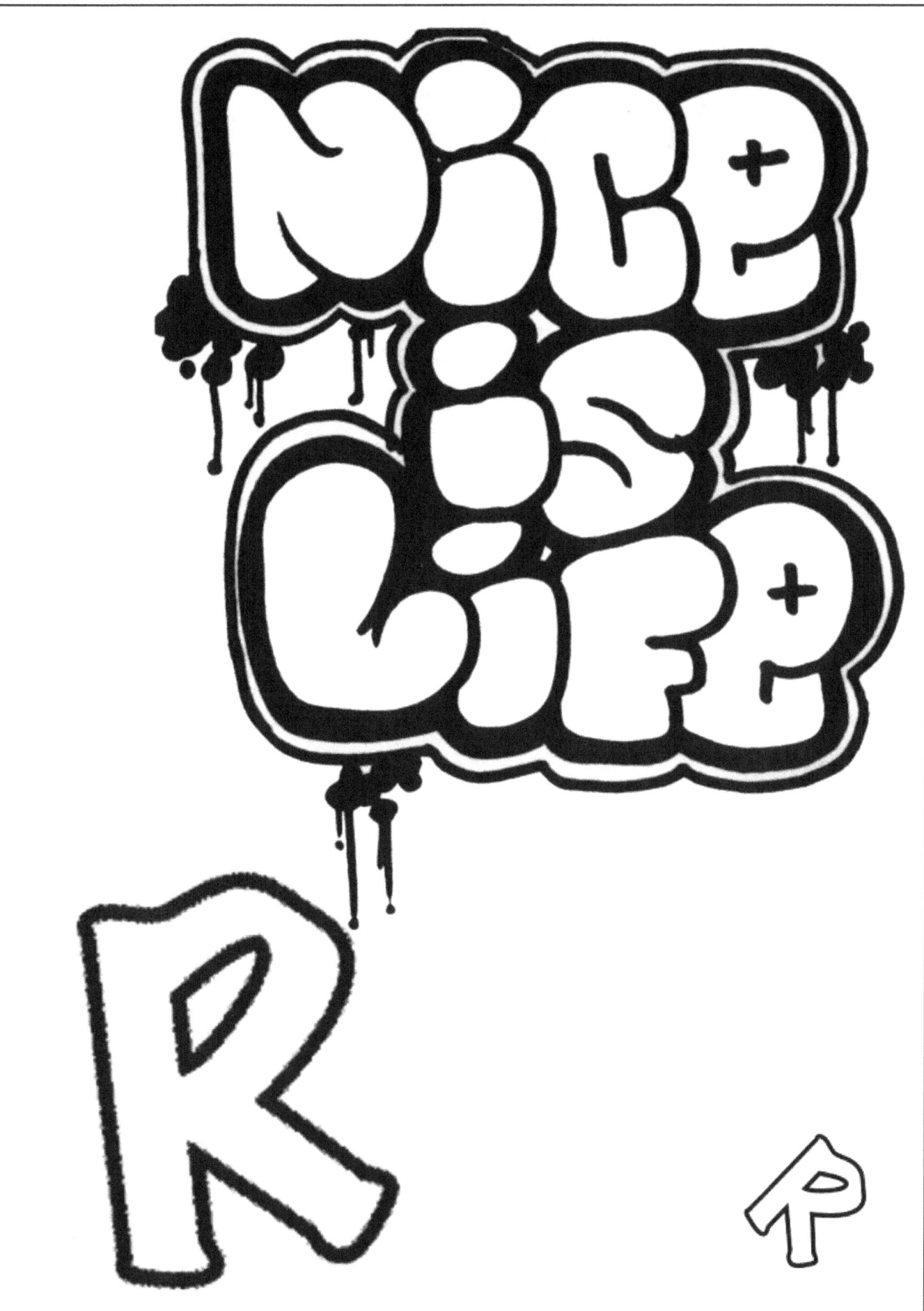

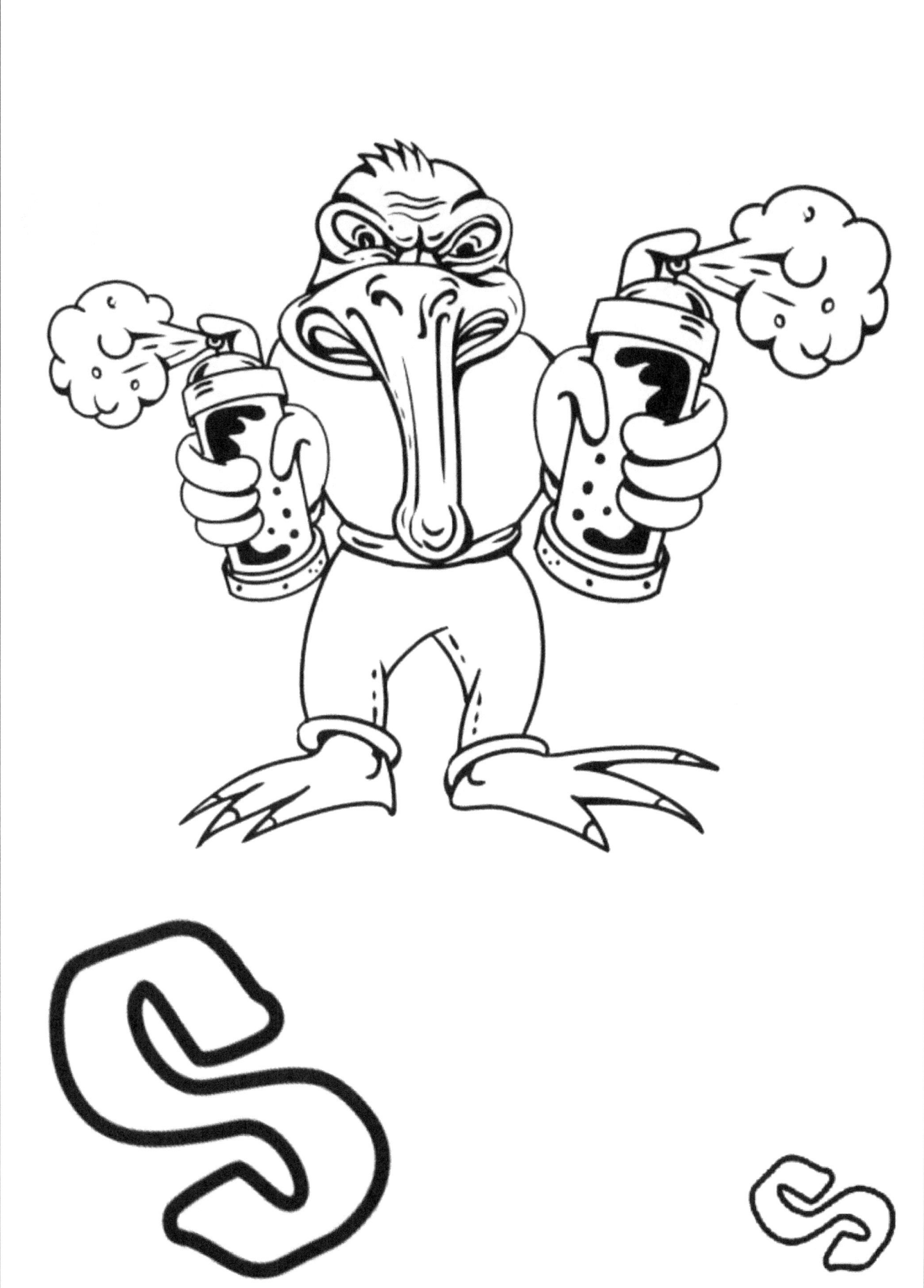

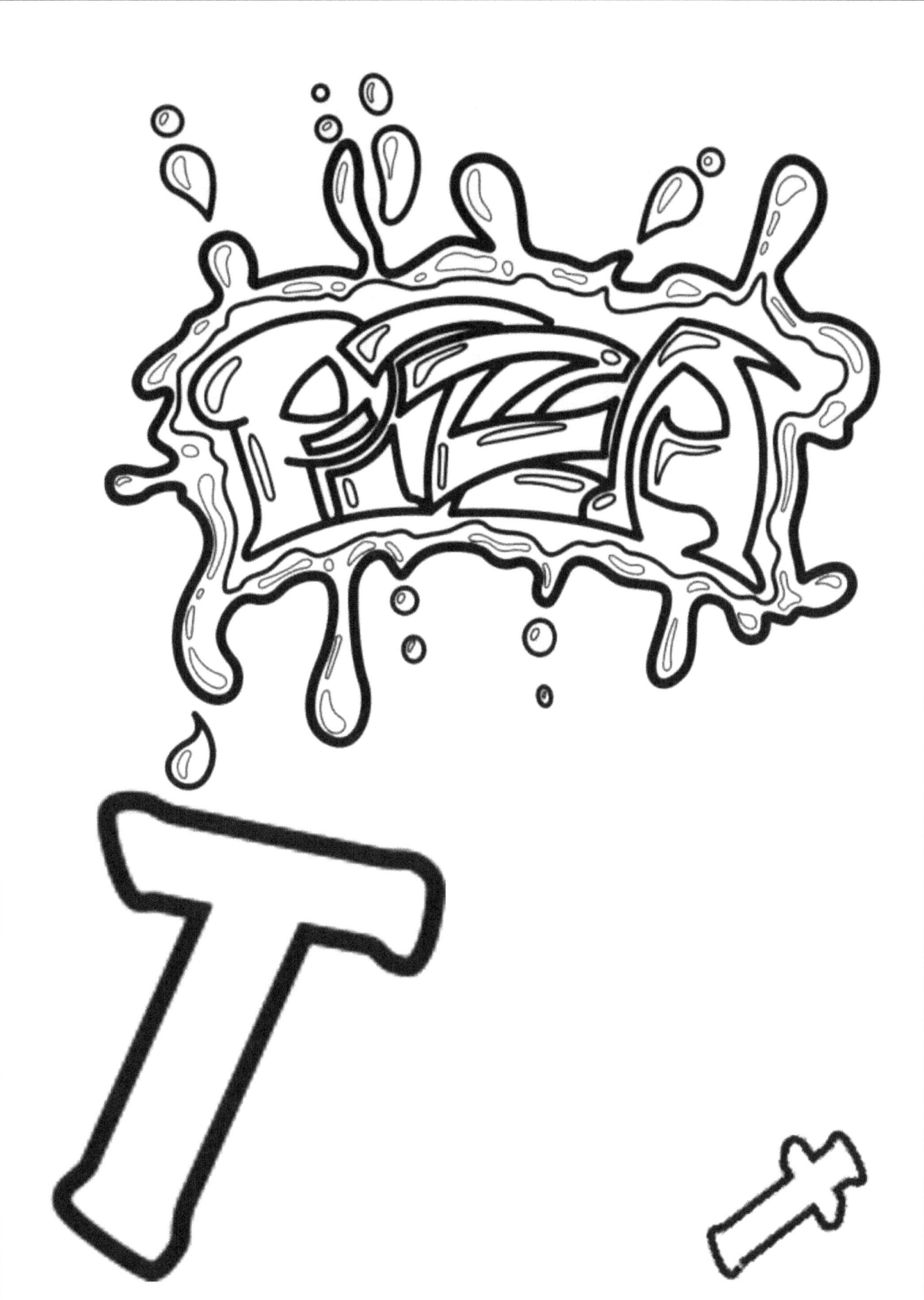

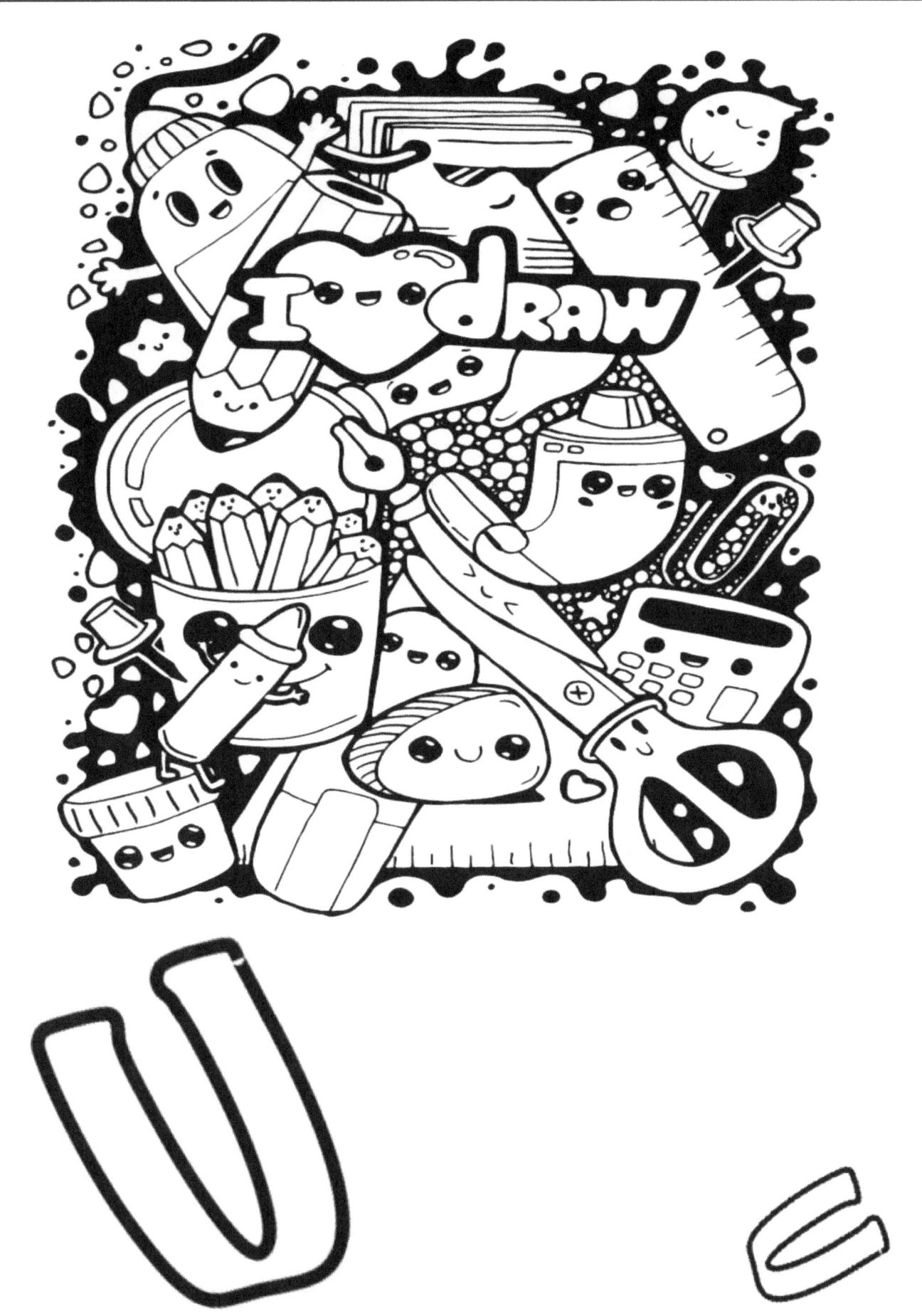

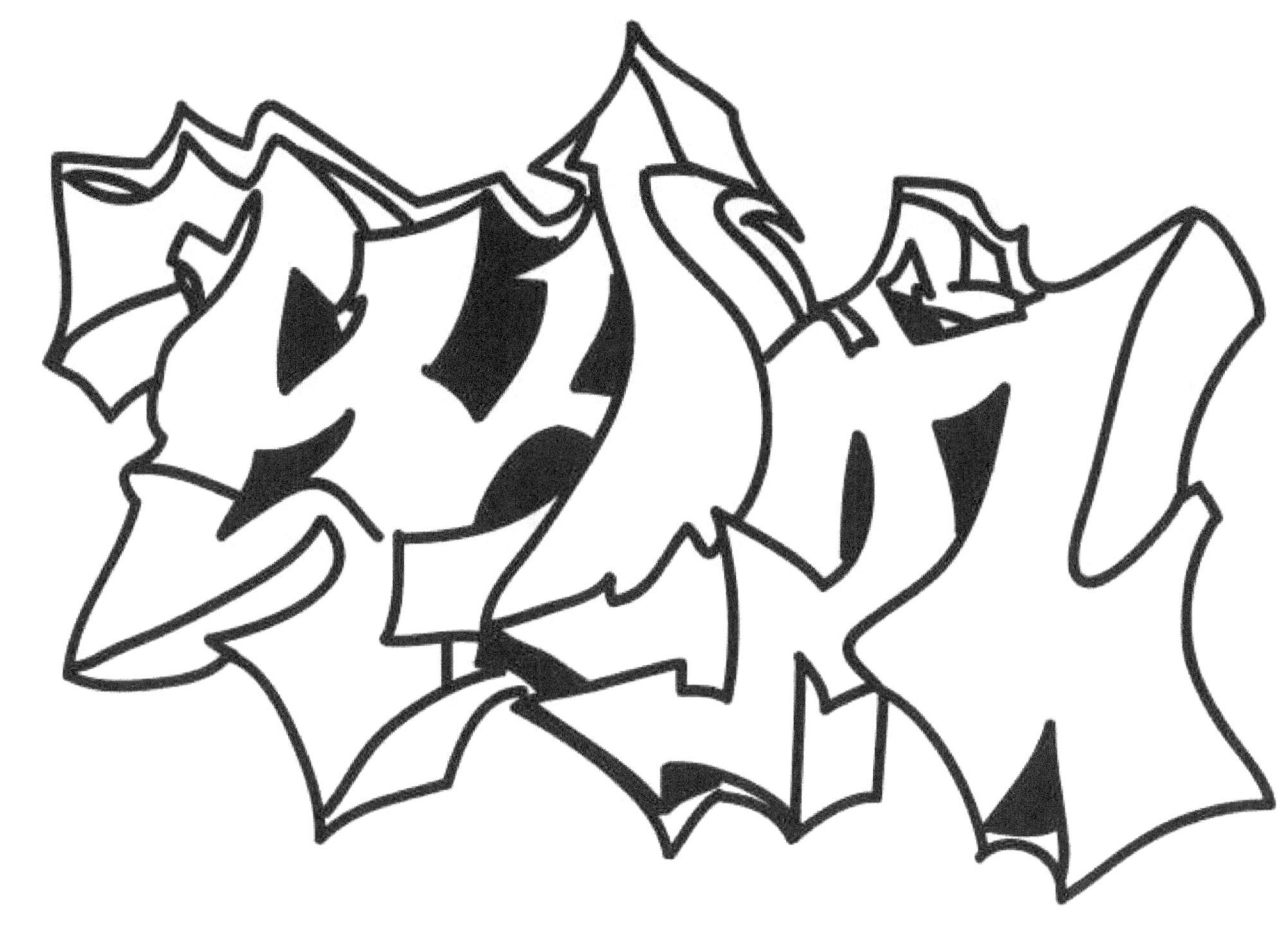

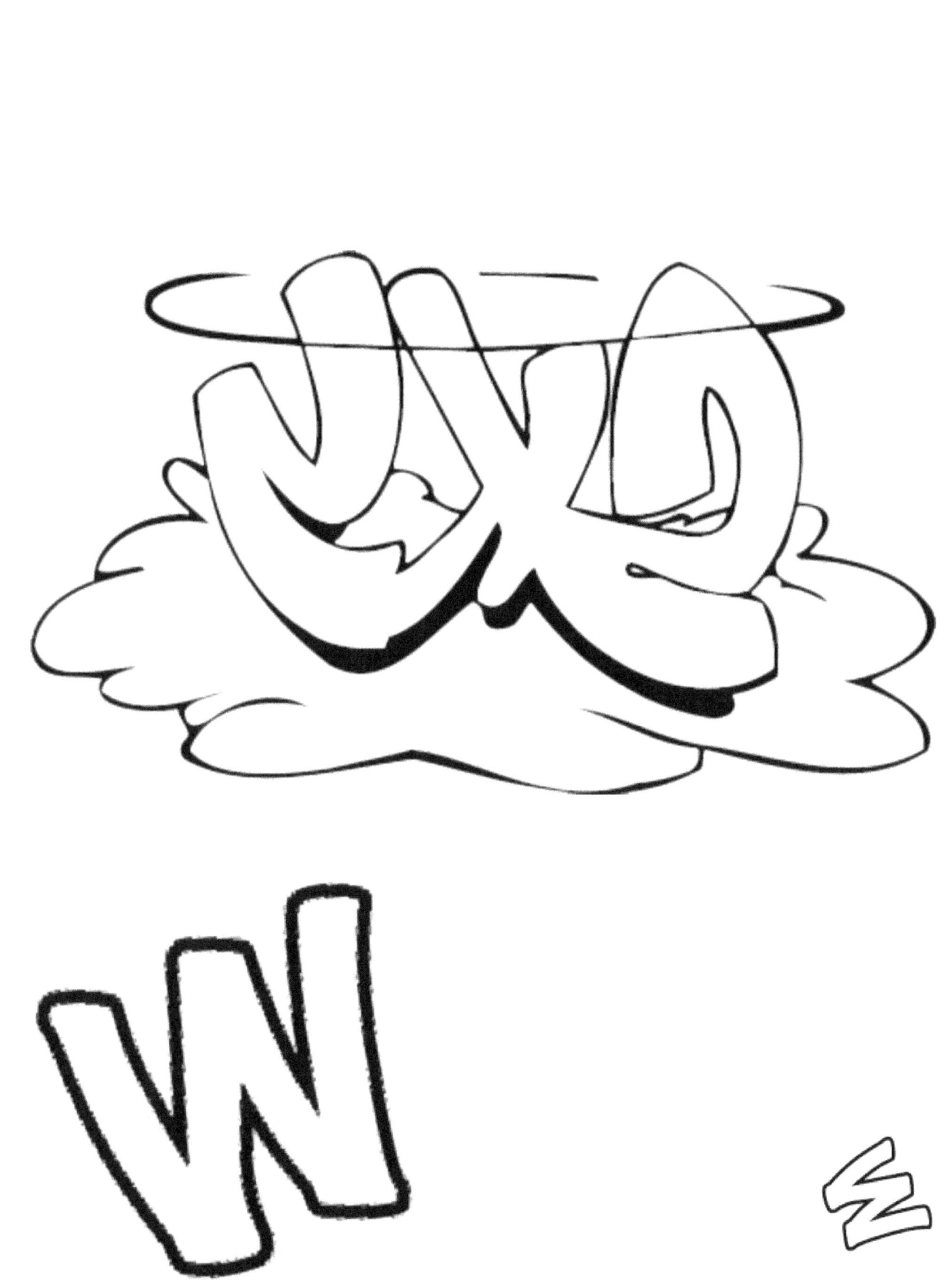

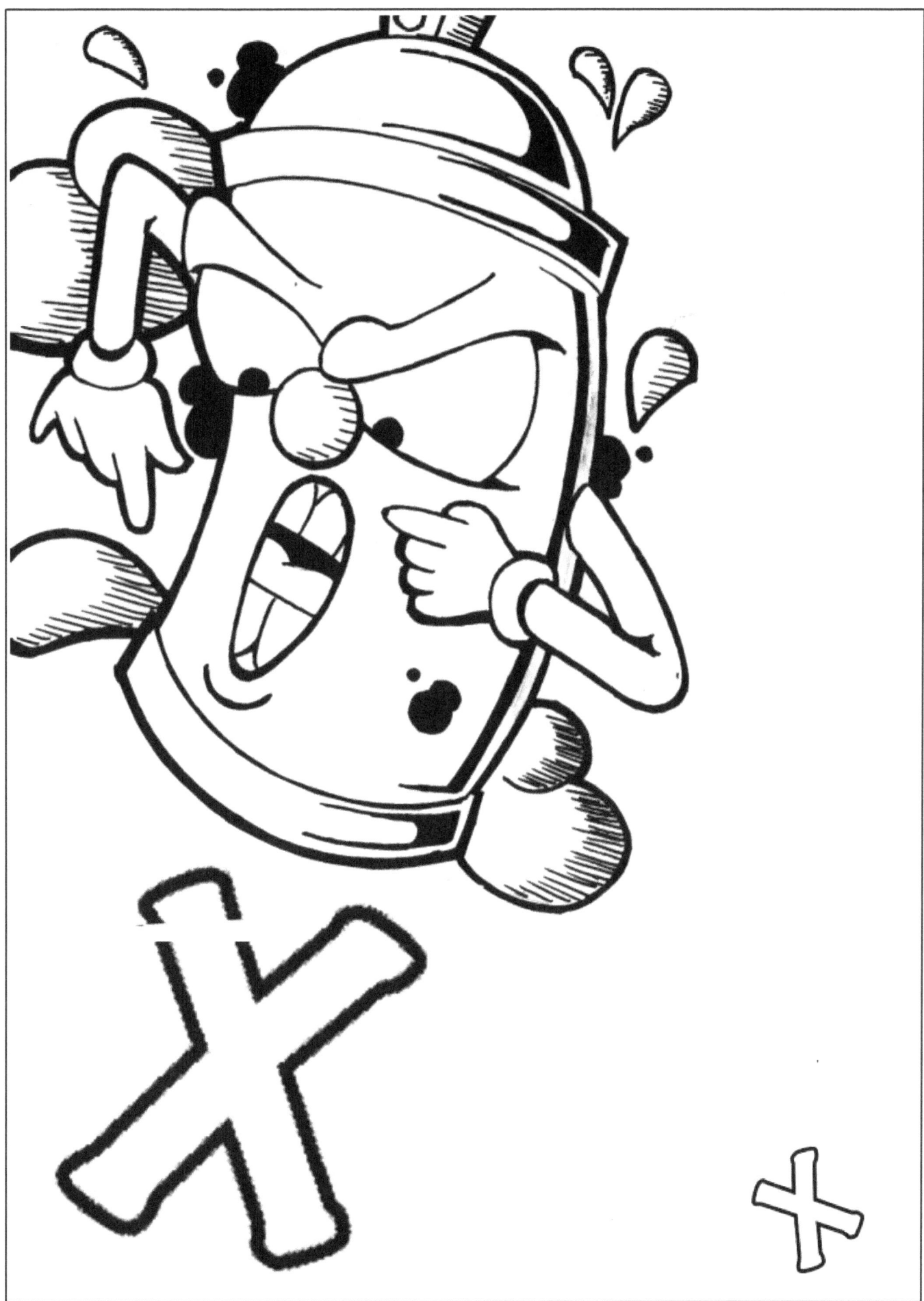

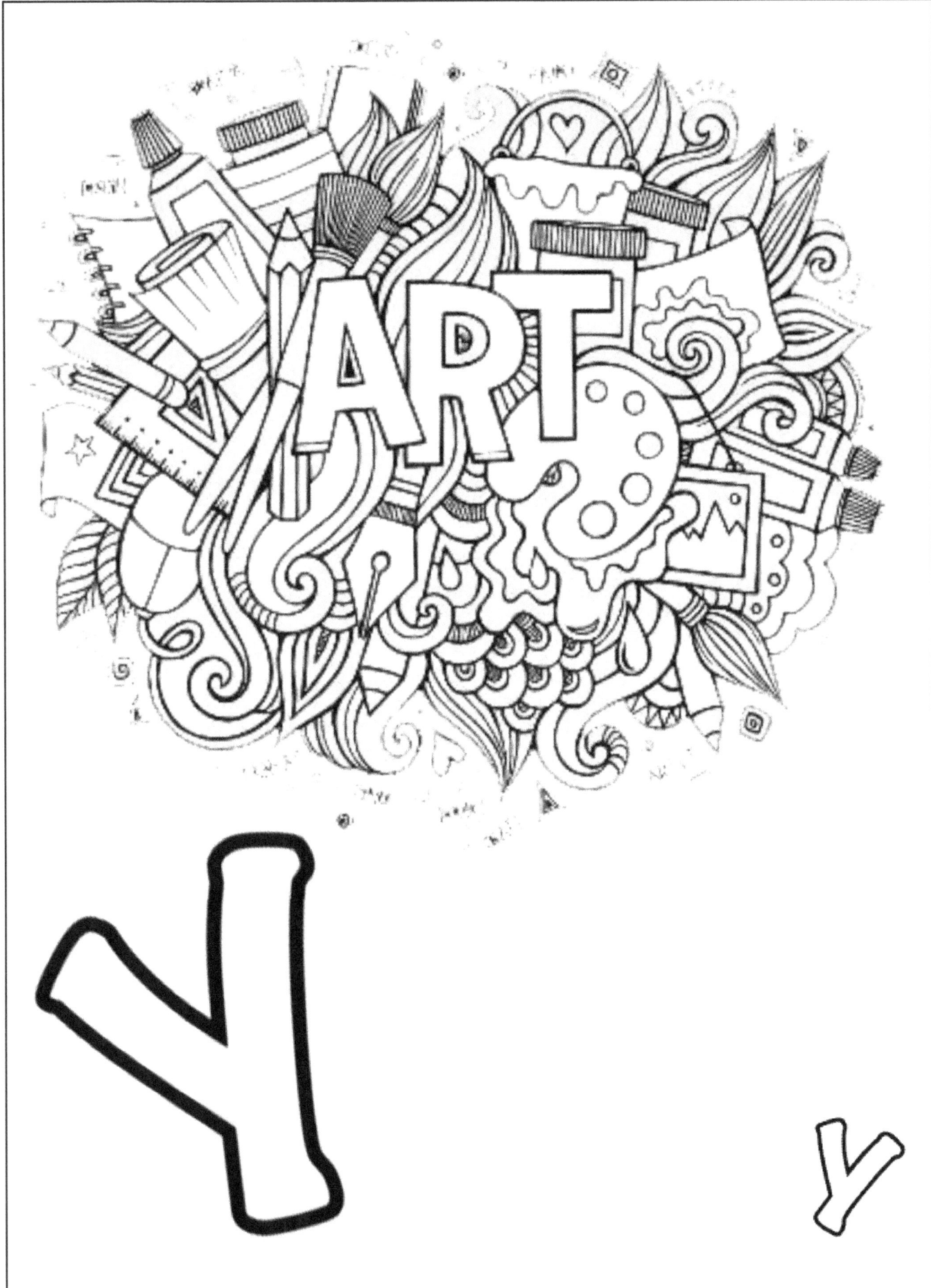

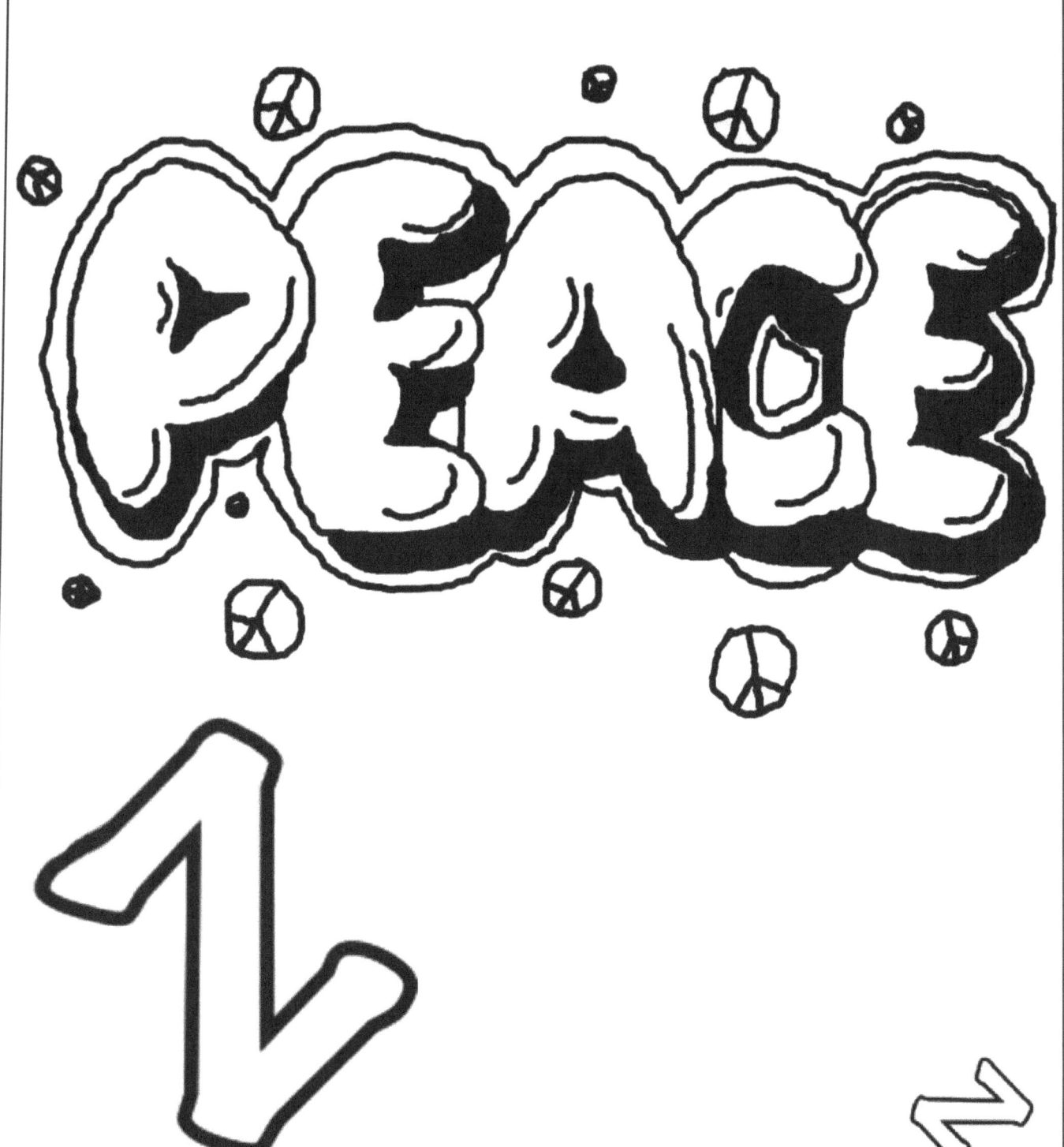

www.ingramcontent.com/pod-product-compliance
Lightning Source LLC
Chambersburg PA
CBHW080535220526
45465CB00006B/2713